On the Move

THE STORY OF A
HELICOPTER

MW01152686

Kingfisher Books, Grisewood & Dempsey Ltd,
Elsley House, 24–30 Great Titchfield Street,
London W1P 7AD

First published in 1990 by Kingfisher Books

Reprinted 1990

BRITISH LIBRARY CATALOGUING IN PUBLICATION DATA
Royston, Angela
   Helicopter.
   1. Helicopters
   I. Title   II. Dupasquier, Philippe   III. Series
   629.133352
ISBN 0 86272 537 2

With thanks to Squadron Leader D J Carey and Flight
Lieutenant J K Moody of RAF, Manston, Kent

Edited by Veronica Pennycook
Designed by Ben White
Cover design by Terry Woodley
Phototypeset by Southern Positives and Negatives (SPAN),
Lingfield, Surrey
Printed in Spain

On the Move

THE STORY OF A
HELICOPTER

By Angela Royston
Illustrated by Philippe Dupasquier

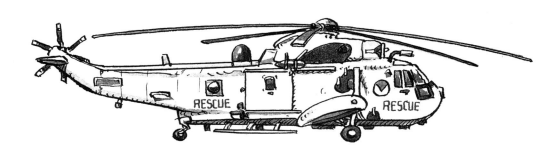

Kingfisher Books

The helicopter in this story is a Sea King. Different types of helicopter are used for different work. Sea Kings are often used for rescues from the air.

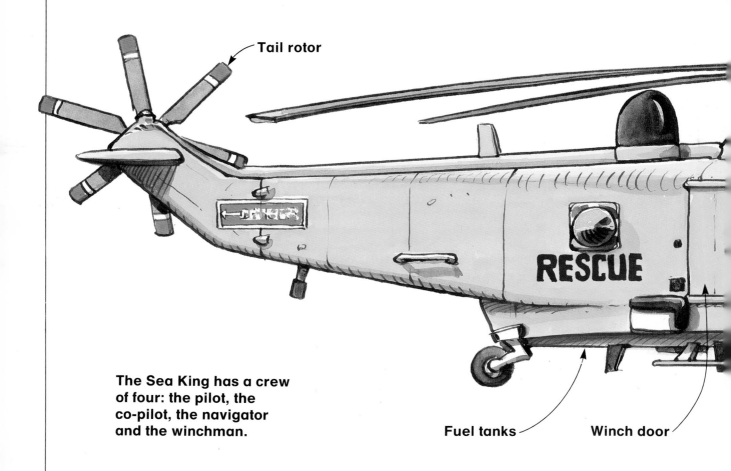

Tail rotor

RESCUE

The Sea King has a crew of four: the pilot, the co-pilot, the navigator and the winchman.

Fuel tanks — **Winch door**

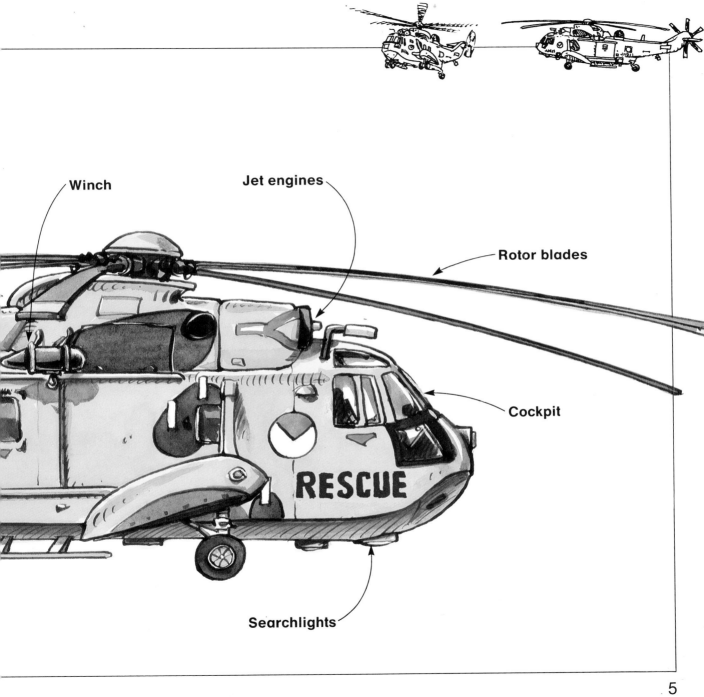

Winch

Jet engines

Rotor blades

Cockpit

RESCUE

Searchlights

The helicopter waits at the airbase for an emergency call. It is ready to fly at any moment to rescue people from cliffs or mountains, from ships or the sea. But this morning there are no calls, so the four crew members work in the office.

After lunch the crew put on their helmets, life jackets and gloves and go out to the helicopter. They fly every day to practise different kinds of rescues. Today John will come with them so they can practise lifting him from a life raft in the sea.

Gary, the pilot, starts the engines and the rotor
blades whirl. He pulls a lever to make the helicopter
rise slowly. Then Gary steers it towards the sea.
The engines are so noisy that the crew use
microphones in their helmets to talk to each other.

"Here's a clear patch of sea where we can lower John," says Chris, the co-pilot. John fastens the life raft on to his back and then clips himself on to the hook at the end of the winch cable. Steve opens the winch door and lowers him down slowly.

When John reaches the sea he unhooks himself. He quickly unpacks the life raft and inflates it. Now it is Mike's turn. Steve pulls the winch cable back in and fastens the hook to Mike's harness.

Steve lowers Mike towards the sea. When Mike
lands on the life raft, he fastens John to his harness
and signals to Steve in the helicopter hovering
above. Steve then hauls the two men up together.

They practise rescuing John several more times,
before they pull the life raft into the helicopter and
fly back to the airbase. "Sea King 166, you can
land now," says Air Traffic Control to Gary on the
radio. Gary brings the helicopter slowly down.

As soon as the helicopter lands, the ground crew
come over. They wash the salt water off the winch
cable and oil it to stop it from rusting. They refill
the fuel tanks and check the engines. The helicopter
is soon ready to fly again.

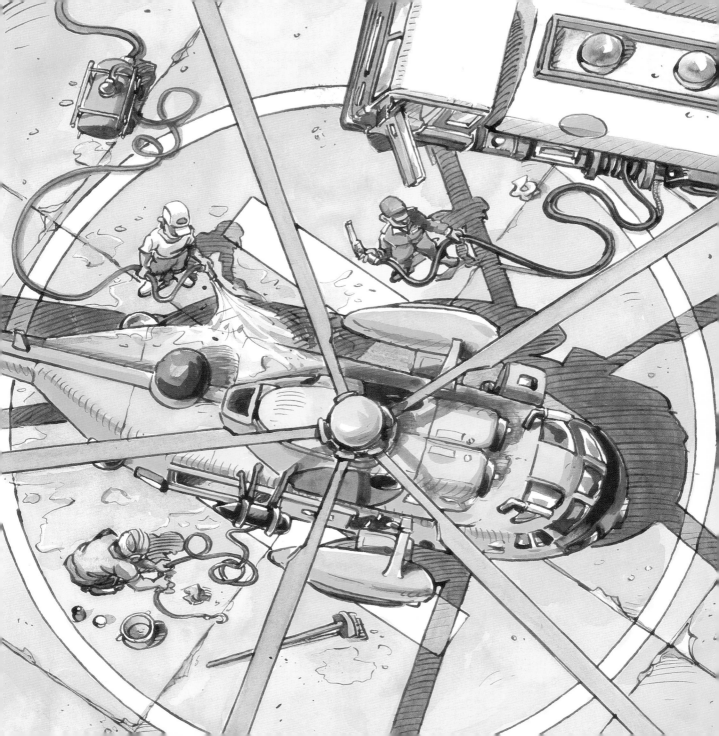

Suddenly the red emergency telephone rings. Chris answers it. "A seaman on a cargo ship has been badly crushed. He must go to hospital at once." The coastguard tells Chris the ship's position.

It is evening and getting colder. All the crew quickly put on immersion suits to keep them warm.

They run to the helicopter to start the engines and to check they have everything they need.

Seven minutes after the telephone rang the helicopter takes off. Chris taps the ship's position into the computer. Now Gary can use the compass to find the ship.

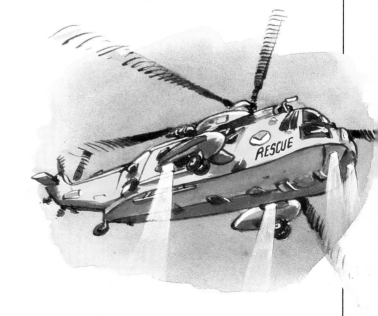

It is getting dark so Gary and Chris cannot see clearly outside. The compass shows them which way to go and Steve watches for the ship on the radar screen. "Ship close by on right," Steve says. Chris turns on the searchlights and Steve opens the winch door.

While the helicopter circles, Steve and Mike peer down into the beam of light. "There it is, 100 metres on the right!" shouts Mike. Chris radios to the coastguard that they have found the ship.

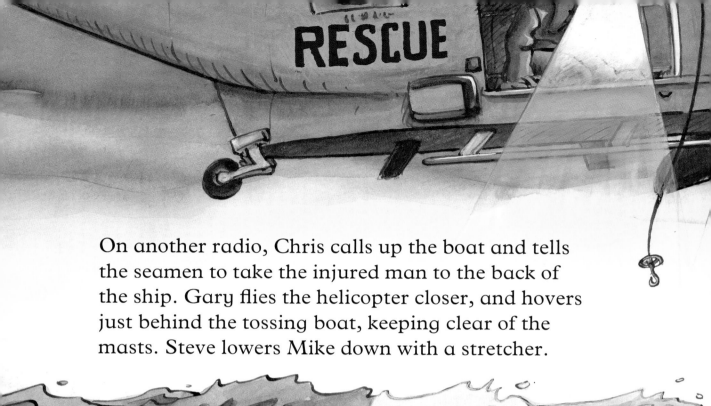

On another radio, Chris calls up the boat and tells the seamen to take the injured man to the back of the ship. Gary flies the helicopter closer, and hovers just behind the tossing boat, keeping clear of the masts. Steve lowers Mike down with a stretcher.

Gary brings the helicopter forward a little and
Mike's feet touch the deck. He fastens the injured
seaman on to the stretcher and Steve winches them
up together. "Winchman and casualty on board,"
reports Steve and he shuts the winch door.

Gary turns the helicopter back towards land while Chris radios the coastguard. They decide that the helicopter should go to the nearest hospital. A space is cleared in the hospital car park so the helicopter can land. Two cars light the landing spot.

The police and a fire engine wait nearby in case there is an accident. As the helicopter gets close Gary turns on the searchlights. He brings the helicopter gently down to land and the injured seaman is rushed into hospital.

The helicopter takes off and flies back to the airbase. At once the ground crew get it ready to fly again, then they tow it into the shelter of the hangar for the night.

There are no more emergency calls that night so both air and ground crews get some sleep. Early the next morning the helicopter is towed out on to the tarmac ready for that day's crews to take over.

Some Special Words

Air Traffic Control A group of people who control where and when aircraft can fly.

Airbase A place where aircraft can take off and land.

Cable Strong wire rope.

Casualty An injured person.

Coastguard A person who keeps watch on a stretch of coast.

Compass An instrument which shows in which direction you are going.

Hangar A large building in which aircraft are kept.

Harness Straps which go around a person and can then fasten on to something else.

Immersion suits Overalls which the air crew wear over their flying suits to keep them warm and dry.

Life jacket A plastic jacket filled with air which keeps a person afloat in the water.

Life raft A raft which cannot sink. It is often made of wood or plastic filled with air.

Radar An instrument which detects ships and large objects and shows their position on a screen.

Winch A way of pulling in and letting out rope using a wheel.

Winchman A person who is lowered by winch to rescue a casualty.